LAYERS OF LEARNING

YEAR ONE • UNIT SEVENTEEN

CELTS
EUROPE
FLOWERING PLANTS
JEWELRY

HooDoo Publishing
United States of America
©2014 Layers of Learning
Copies of maps or activities may be made for a particular family or classroom.
ISBN 978-1495258749

UNITS AT A GLANCE: TOPICS FOR ALL FOUR YEARS OF THE LAYERS OF LEARNING PROGRAM

1	History	Geography	Science	The Arts
1	Mesopotamia	Maps & Globes	Planets	Cave Paintings
2	Egypt	Map Keys	Stars	Egyptian Art
3	Europe	Global Grids	Earth & Moon	Crafts
4	Ancient Greece	Wonders	Satellites	Greek Art
5	Babylon	Mapping People	Humans in Space	Poetry
6	The Levant	Physical Earth	Laws of Motion	List Poems
7	Phoenicians	Oceans	Motion	Moral Stories
8	Assyrians	Deserts	Fluids	Rhythm
9	Persians	Arctic	Waves	Melody
10	Ancient China	Forests	Machines	Chinese Art
11	Early Japan	Mountains	States of Matter	Line & Shape
12	Arabia	Rivers & Lakes	Atoms	Color & Value
13	Ancient India	Grasslands	Elements	Texture & Form
14	Ancient Africa	Africa	Bonding	African Tales
15	First North Americans	North America	Salts	Creative Kids
16	Ancient South America	South America	Plants	South American Art
17	Celts	Europe	Flowering Plants	Jewelry
18	Roman Republic	Asia	Trees	Roman Art
19	Christianity	Australia & Oceania	Simple Plants	Instruments
20	Roman Empire	You Explore	Fungi	Composing Music

2	History	Geography	Science	The Arts
1	Byzantines	Turkey	Climate & Seasons	Byzantine Art
2	Barbarians	Ireland	Forecasting	Illumination
3	Islam	Arabian Peninsula	Clouds & Precipitation	Creative Kids
4	Vikings	Norway	Special Effects	Viking Art
5	Anglo Saxons	Britain	Wild Weather	King Arthur Tales
6	Charlemagne	France	Cells and DNA	Carolingian Art
7	Normans	Nigeria	Skeletons	Canterbury Tales
8	Feudal System	Germany	Muscles, Skin, & Cardiopulmonary	Gothic Art
9	Crusades	Balkans	Digestive & Senses	Religious Art
10	Burgundy, Venice, Spain	Switzerland	Nerves	Oil Paints
11	Wars of the Roses	Russia	Health	Minstrels & Plays
12	Eastern Europe	Hungary	Metals	Printmaking
13	African Kingdoms	Mali	Carbon Chem	Textiles
14	Asian Kingdoms	Southeast Asia	Non-metals	Vivid Language
15	Mongols	Caucasus	Gases	Fun With Poetry
16	Medieval China & Japan	China	Electricity	Asian Arts
17	Pacific Peoples	Micronesia	Circuits	Arts of the Islands
18	American Peoples	Canada	Technology	Indian Legends
19	The Renaissance	Italy	Magnetism	Renaissance Art I
20	Explorers	Caribbean Sea	Motors	Renaissance Art II

3	History	Geography	Science	The Arts
1	Age of Exploration	Argentina and Chile	Classification & Insects	Fairy Tales
2	The Ottoman Empire	Egypt and Libya	Reptiles & Amphibians	Poetry
3	Mogul Empire	Pakistan & Afghanistan	Fish	Mogul Arts
4	Reformation	Angola & Zambia	Birds	Reformation Art
5	Renaissance England	Tanzania & Kenya	Mammals & Primates	Shakespeare
6	Thirty Years' War	Spain	Sound	Baroque Music
7	The Dutch	Netherlands	Light & Optics	Baroque Art I
8	France	Indonesia	Bending Light	Baroque Art II
9	The Enlightenment	Korean Pen.	Color	Art Journaling
10	Russia & Prussia	Central Asia	History of Science	Watercolors
11	Conquistadors	Baltic States	Igneous Rocks	Creative Kids
12	Settlers	Peru & Bolivia	Sedimentary Rocks	Native American Art
13	13 Colonies	Central America	Metamorphic Rocks	Settler Sayings
14	Slave Trade	Brazil	Gems & Minerals	Colonial Art
15	The South Pacific	Australasia	Fossils	Principles of Art
16	The British in India	India	Chemical Reactions	Classical Music
17	Boston Tea Party	Japan	Reversible Reactions	Folk Music
18	Founding Fathers	Iran	Compounds & Solutions	Rococo
19	Declaring Independence	Samoa and Tonga	Oxidation & Reduction	Creative Crafts I
20	The American Revolution	South Africa	Acids & Bases	Creative Crafts II

4	History	Geography	Science	The Arts
1	American Government	USA	Heat & Temperature	Patriotic Music
2	Expanding Nation	Pacific States	Motors & Engines	Tall Tales
3	Industrial Revolution	U.S. Landscapes	Energy	Romantic Art I
4	Revolutions	Mountain West States	Energy Sources	Romantic Art II
5	Africa	U.S. Political Maps	Energy Conversion	Impressionism I
6	The West	Southwest States	Earth Structure	Impressionism II
7	Civil War	National Parks	Plate Tectonics	Post-Impressionism
8	World War I	Plains States	Earthquakes	Expressionism
9	Totalitarianism	U.S. Economics	Volcanoes	Abstract Art
10	Great Depression	Heartland States	Mountain Building	Kinds of Art
11	World War II	Symbols and Landmarks	Chemistry of Air & Water	War Art
12	Modern East Asia	The South States	Food Chemistry	Modern Art
13	India's Independence	People of America	Industry	Pop Art
14	Israel	Appalachian States	Chemistry of Farming	Modern Music
15	Cold War	U.S. Territories	Chemistry of Medicine	Free Verse
16	Vietnam War	Atlantic States	Food Chains	Photography
17	Latin America	New England States	Animal Groups	Latin American Art
18	Civil Rights	Home State Study	Instincts	Theater & Film
19	Technology	Home State Study II	Habitats	Architecture
20	Terrorism	America in Review	Conservation	Creative Kids

Unit 1-17 Printable Pack

This unit includes printables at the end. To make life easier for you we also created digital printable packs for each unit. To retrieve your printable pack for Unit 1-17, please visit

www.layers-of-learning.com/digital-printable-packs/

Put the printable pack in your shopping cart and use this coupon code:

0118UNIT1-17

Your printable pack will be free.

LAYERS OF LEARNING INTRODUCTION

This is part of a series of units in the Layers of Learning homeschool curriculum, including the subjects of history, geography, science, and the arts. Children from 1st through 12th can participate in the same curriculum at the same time – family school style.

The units are intended to be used in order as the basis of a complete curriculum (once you add in a systematic math, reading, and writing program). You begin with Year 1 Unit 1 no matter what ages your children are. Spend about 2 weeks on each unit. You pick and choose the activities within the unit that appeal to you and read the books from the book list that are available to you or find others on the same topic from your library. We highly recommend that you use the timeline in every history section as the backbone. Then flesh out your learning with reading and activities that highlight the topics you think are the most important.

Alternatively, you can use the units as activity ideas to supplement another curriculum in any order you wish. You can still use them with all ages of children at the same time.

When you've finished with Year One, move on to Year Two, Year Three, and Year Four. Then begin again with Year One and work your way through the years again. Now your children will be older, reading more involved books, and writing more in depth. When you have completed the sequence for the second time, you start again on it for the third and final time. If your student began with Layers of Learning in 1st grade and stayed with it all the way through she would go through the four year rotation three times, firmly cementing the information in her mind in ever increasing depth. At each level you should expect increasing amounts of outside reading and writing. High schoolers in particular should be reading extensively, and if possible, participating in discussion groups.

☺ ☻ ☻ These icons will guide you in spotting activities and books that are appropriate for the age of child you are working with. But if you think an activity is too juvenile or too difficult for your kids, adjust accordingly. The icons are not there as rules, just guides.

☺ GRADES 1-4
☻ GRADES 5-8
☻ GRADES 9-12

Within each unit we share:
- EXPLORATIONS, activities relating to the topic;
- EXPERIMENTS, usually associated with science topics;
- EXPEDITIONS, field trips;
- EXPLANATIONS, teacher helps or educational philosophies.

In the sidebars we also include Additional Layers, Famous Folks, Fabulous Facts, On the Web, and other extra related topics that can take you off on tangents, exploring the world and your interests with a bit more freedom. The curriculum will always be there to pull you back on track when you're ready.

You can learn more about how to use this curriculum at www.layers-of-learning.com/layers-of-learning-program/

UNIT SEVENTEEN
CELTS – EUROPE – FLOWERING PLANTS – JEWELRY

"The simplest schoolboy is now familiar with truths for which Archimedes would have sacrificed his life."
-Ernest Renan, French philosopher

	LIBRARY LIST:
HISTORY	Search for: Celts, Book of Kells ☺ ☺ ☻ Celtic Fairy Tales by Neil Phillip. Illustrations on every page and simplified tales make this entertaining. ☺ ☻ Color Your Own Book of Kells by Marty Noble. A coloring book. ☺ ☻ Ancient Celtic Festivals and How We Celebrate Them Today by Clare Walker Leslie. Connects the ancient Celts to who we are today. ☺ ☻ Life in Celtic Times by A.G. Smith. A Dover coloring book. Detailed pictures and descriptions on each page. ☺ ☻ Celtic Design Coloring Book by Ed Sibbett Jr. Celtic knots, illustrations, letters and so on, including images from the Book of Kells in a coloring book. ☺ The Ancient Celts by Patricia Calvert. ☺ Celts by Hazel Mary Martell. Fascinating illustrations accompany the informative text which includes daily life of the Celts and a few Celtic myths. ☺ Cut-Throat Celts by Terry Deary. Part of the Horrible Histories series; kids just eat these up. ☺ ☻ Favorite Celtic Fairy Tales by Joseph Jacobs. A Dover book, this is very affordable. Contains eight tales and a few black and white illustrations. ☻ The Chronicles of the Celts by Peter Berresford Ellis. A modern retelling of ancient Celtic myths by a novelist. ☻ The World of the Celts by Simon James. Interesting read and over 300 illustrations. ☻ The Celts: A Very Short Introduction by Barry Cunliff. It is short and to the point, plus readily accessible of the lay reader, but also based on scholarship.
GEOGRAPHY	Search for: Europe ☻ Europe by Madeline Donaldson. ☺ ☻ Traditional Folk Costumes of Europe Paper Dolls by Kathy Allert. Paper punch out dolls in colorful costumes. ☺ ☻ Europe by Sandra Newman. ☺ ☻ Explore Europe by Bobbie Kalman. ☺ ☻ Europe By David Peterson. ☺ ☻ The Story of Europe by H.E. Marshall. Really a history book, valuable for getting a feel for the continent as a whole and also a perfect introduction to the medieval period. ☻ The Europe Book from Lonely Planet. A coffee table photo book.

SCIENCE

Search for: flowering plants, flowers, plants, botany, field guides

☺ ☻ ☻ American Wildflowers Coloring Book by Paul Kennedy.

☻ How Flowers Grow by Emma Helbrough.

☻ The Flower Alphabet Book by Jerry Pallotta. Fabulous and accurate illustrations of 26 flowers from A to Z.

☻ The Reason For a Flower by Ruth Heller.

☻ The Life Cycle of a Flower by Bobbie Kalman. Old earth dates, evolutionary content.

☻ Planting a Rainbow by Lois Ehlert. Teaches children how to plant and grow a garden of flowers.

☻ A Little Guide to Wild Flowers by Charlotte Voake. A field guide for very young children.

☺ ☻ Listen To The Flowers: Ten Flower Stories For Children by Jill Ann Williams. Fanciful stories told from the point of view of the flower.

☺ ☻ How to Draw Flowers by Barbara Soloff-Levy.

☺ ☻ Garden Flowers Coloring Book by Stefan Bernath.

☺ ☻ The Facts About Flowering Plants by Rebecca Hunter.

☻ Flowers by David Burnie.

☻ Classifying Flowering Plants by Francine Galco. Contains evolutionary content.

☺ ☻ Wildflowers: A Golden Guide by Alexander C. Martin and Herbert S. Zimm. A field guide to American wildflowers.

☻ Flowering Plant Families of the World by V.H. Heywood, et. al. A colorfully and copiously illustrated reference book of flowering plants arranged in families.

☻ Plant Identification Terminology by Melinda and James G. Harris. The most difficult aspect of plant identification and botany in general is mastering the hundreds of technical terms used when describing plants. A must have for students interested in botany or ecology.

☻ Botany for Gardeners by Brian Capon. A college level botany book for everyone.

THE ARTS

Search for: jewelry

☺ ☻ Paper Beads By Anne Akers Johnson. A Klutz book with instructions and materials all in one for a complete kit.

☺ ☻ Hemp Jewelry by Judy Anne Sadler and June Bradford.

☺ ☻ Super Simple Jewelry by Karen Latchana Kenney.

☺ ☻ Artful Jewelry by Jo Packham.

☺ ☻ Friendship Bracelets by Laura Torres. A Klutz kit with all the materials and instructions needed. Look for other Klutz titles.

☺ ☻ Scoubidou: A Book of Lanyard and Lacing by Karen Phillips. Klutz book with all the materials and instructions to make bracelets, key chains, fancy flip flops, and more.

HISTORY: CELTS

Fabulous Fact

"Celts" is pronounced with a hard "c" sound like kelts, not selts.

Famous Folks

Hallstatt, the site thought to be the oldest Celtic civilization, was discovered in 1846 by Johann Georg Ramsaur, an Austrian mine operator.

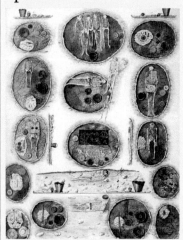

Ramsaur was put in charge of excavating the cemetery at Hallstatt. Above you see one of the watercolor paintings of grave sites which he had commissioned.

Fabulous Fact

The Celts had a written language, but very little of their writings have been found.

The Celts weren't a nation. They were distinct tribes and villages and small kingdoms with similar culture, similar language, and possibly common ancestors. Archaeologists believe the Celtic way of life began at Hallstatt in Austria and spread from there across much of Europe.

They farmed, fished, and raised flocks of animals. They settled in small, self-governing villages, which expanded as surrounding areas were conquered. The head of the village was the chief, or king, who sat with a council to decide important matters. The kings and nobles were all warriors. In some cases the women went to war and served as kings as well. There were a few tribes that were always ruled by women. Kings among the Celts were usually elected. The position wasn't hereditary.

Bards traveled from village to village bringing news and telling tales, singing songs, and reciting poems for entertainment. A bard was treated like royalty. Besides royalty, nobles, and bards, everybody else was part of the lower class – the peasants. There were slaves as well, some who had been captured in war or sold for payment of debt by their families. Slavery was hereditary.

Celt religion was ruled by druid priests. They believed that all of nature, including animals, plants, and rocks had spirits. They offered sacrifices to keep the gods happy – sometimes gold, weapons, animals, and even humans.

A Celt home was one large room built of either wood or stone and topped with a thatched roof. They were usually circular in shape with a central fire for warmth and cooking. They were metal workers who made swords, axes, cooking pots, and fine jewelry. They were also warriors who fought fiercely in battle against neighboring tribes. Sometimes they built hill forts from earth to protect their property and helpless members of their community. They were eventually conquered by the Romans except for Ireland, Scotland, and Wales. When the Romans converted to Christianity, so did the Celtic people.

😊 😊 😊 **EXPLORATION: Make A Timeline**
Printable timeline squares can be found at the end of this unit.
- •700-500 BC Hallstatt Celtic culture emerges
- •600 BC Celts begin to trade with Mediterranean, Britain is first mentioned as "Albion"
- •500 BC Celts arrive in Hibernia (Ireland) from the Iberian Peninsula
- •400 BC Celts attack the Etruscans
- •390 BC Celts sack Rome, think about occupying the land, are disgusted by the filth, and demand a ransom instead.
- •279 BC Celts invade Greece
- •275 BC Celts from Gaul move to Asia Minor, calling it Galatia
- •230 BC Galatians defeated by Greeks
- •200 BC Celts establish permanent hill forts
- •121 BC Rome begins to invade and conquer Celtic Lands
- •70 BC Druids from the Middle East arrive in Britain and take over the ruling class
- •58-51 BC Julius Caesar defeats Gaul
- •54 BC Romans gain a foothold in Britain
- •79 AD Roman consolidation of Britain, not including Scotland and Wales
- •122 AD Hadrian's Wall built
- •313 AD Christianity officially brought to Rome and Roman held Celtic lands
- •367 AD Hadrian's Wall falls and Roman decline begins
- •410 AD Romans abandon Britain. Celtic people left to defend themselves. They are overrun by Saxons, but resist under a King called Arthur.
- •Celtic cultures in Ireland, Scotland and Wales are left intact.

Additional Layer

Castell Henllys is a reconstructed Celtic village built on top of the excavated remains in south Wales.

Photograph by Ruth Jowett and shared on wikimedia commons.

Search the web for more images and information.

On The Web

Visit this site:

http://www.bbc.co.uk/wales/celts/

You can watch interactive videos about the Celts, learn more, and make crafts.

Additional Layer

Celts worshiped many gods. Most of them we have no record of since we have to rely on Roman writings for the most part. We do know about Teutatis, Taranis and Lugus, three of the major gods. We also believe they worshiped nature spirits and believed that everything in nature had a spirit.

Explanation

This simple little whisper phone, made of pvc pipe, is to help emergent readers become better readers.

They've been around forever and have helped lots of kids improve their comprehension skills.

You quietly read into them and the sound gets funneled right to your own ears. They help kids who have trouble focusing to stay on track as they're reading aloud. Kids can hear their words almost as if someone else is reading to them. They hear only themselves even if they're in a noisy room or other people are reading at the same time.

Karen

Additional Layer

Learn more about woad. What is it and when did people use it?

☺ ☺ ☻ EXPLORATION: Celtic Lands Map

Make a map of Celtic lands. Use the Celtic Lands map from the end of this unit. Label the cities of Rome, Delphi, and Hallstatt, which is a major Celtic city situated along the Danube River. Color in the Celtic areas.

Notice the specific labels of the lands where the Celts lived: Hibernia, Britain, Celtiberians, Gaul, and Galatia.

Color in the Celtic areas and make a key.

Celtic Lands

☺ ☺ ☻ EXPLORATION: Celtic Calendar

The Celtic calendar was arranged in a five year cycle with an extra month being inserted every 2 ½ years to realign with the solar calendar. Six five-year cycles made up an age. The start of each new age omitted the additional month at the beginning of Samon, to realign with the solar year. The start of each month was the quarter full moon, when the moon was directly overhead, and the month was divided into two halves, or fortnights of fourteen to fifteen days. There were four main Celtic holidays: Samhain (November 1), Imbolc (February 1), Beltain (May 1), and Lunasa (August 1). There were also four solar days noted by the Celts – the winter and summer solstices and the spring and autumn equinoxes.

Age of 30 yrs →Cycle of 5 Yrs →Year of 12 or 13 months→ Month of 29 or 30 days

Beltane is the start of the light half of the year and the Celtic New Year. It falls around May 1. Two fires would be built and the people and cattle would pass between them to symbolize purification as a start to the new season of fertility. All other fires in the community would be put out and then the home fires would be re-lit from the common fire. Bushes were also decorated with flowers, ribbons and colored egg shells.

Lughnasadh, about August 1st, was the time of the first harvest, the beginning of harvest season. It was a traditional time to marry, to feast, to hold contests of strength and skill and to have a bonfire. It is a celebration to the god Lugh, who was the deity of storms and lightning.

Samhain is the harvest festival and marks the start of the dark half of the year on about November 1st. It is a time when spirits are especially close, and in order to placate those spirits young people would wear costumes or masks, hollow out and decorate turnips with faces, and light bonfires. Samhain has been passed down to us as Halloween.

Imbolc was dedicated to the goddess Brigid and is the festival of the start of spring, falling about February 1st. It was important as the start of lambing season. People would forecast or use divination to determine things like what the weather would be for the coming year, or who so and so would marry, how many children so and so would have and things like that. There would be feasting and candles and a bonfire.

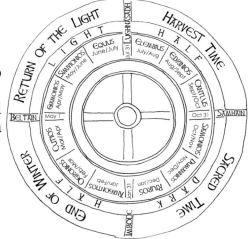

Print out the calendar from the end of this unit and color it. Make each month a different color.

☺ ● EXPLORATION: Celtic Clothes

Dress like a Celt. One piece of purely Celtic jewelry was the torc, a piece of worked and twisted metal worn around the neck. Both women and men wore them. You can make one out of pipe cleaners. Either use metallic pipe cleaners or spray paint four pipe cleaners in metallic paint and let them dry. Twist or braid them together, bending the ends into a ball. Wrap it around your neck. The two ends sit in front below your chin.

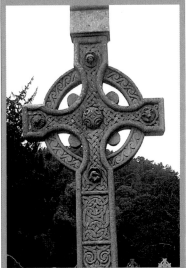

Some say the circle was introduced by St. Patrick to integrate or show the supremacy of Christian belief with traditional sun worship. Others think the circle was purely practical as high crosses, large standing stone crosses, often needed the extra support or they would break.

Sadly, a modern use of the Celtic cross is as a symbol of the racist neo-Nazi movement.

Famous Folks

After the Romans began to invade the Celtic Tribes in Britain, a leader named Caractacus arose and fought bravely against the invaders. He was captured and taken to Rome as a prize of war, but later released. Before he went home he went on a tour of the city.

Caractacus in Rome.

A Roman historian, Cassius Dio, said this:

"Caractacus, a barbarian chieftain who was captured and brought to Rome and later pardoned by Claudius, wandered about the city after his liberation and after beholding its splendor and magnitude he exclaimed: and can you then who have got such possessions and so many of them, still covet our poor huts?"

Why did the Romans want Celtic lands so badly?

Add to your Celtic costume by wearing a long loose fitting brightly colored shirt and loose fitting pants. Tie a belt around your shirt. Wear a cloak in cool weather. If you are a boy, spike your hair with gel (Celts used lime, but you can stick with gel). If you are a girl, braid your hair. Warriors going into battle often used woad, a blue dye, to make patterns on their skin. Make some swirls and geometric patterns on your skin with blue face paint.

☺ ☻ **EXPLORATION: Vercingetorix's Sword**
Vercingetorix (verse-in-jet-or-ix) was a leader of the Averni Tribe in Gaul. He succeeded in uniting the Gaulish tribes against the Roman invaders in 52-41 BC. The Roman leader he fought

against was a general named Julius Caesar who would later ride on his popularity to overthrow the Roman Republic and get himself made a dictator. After a series of exciting battles, Vercingetorix made his last stand at the city of Alesia, where Julius surrounded and besieged the city. The Romans themselves were surrounded by the rest of Gaul as they had not subdued the countryside or surrounding cities. A relief column rode to the aid of Alesia, but the concerted attack of the inner and outer forces failed. In order to spare his people further death and suffering, Vercingetorix surrendered himself to Julius. He was held for five years in a prison in Rome and then was a featured prisoner at Julius' triumphal parade. Immediately afterward he was executed. This battle was pivotal in the downfall of the Celtic tribes in Gaul and essential to the growth of Rome as an empire.

Vercingetorix surrenders to Julius Caesar.
Painting by Lionel Royer, 1899.

Read more about Vercingetorix and his struggle to remain free of Rome. Not all of the Gallic tribes felt this way. Many allied with Rome or surrendered without a fight in order to be part of Rome and its economic and military power. Do you think Vercingetorix was right in resisting or not? Why?

Make Vercingetorix's sword from newspaper, tape, and metallic spray paint.

Take six sheets of newspaper in an even stack and roll up from one corner of the paper. Use a pen placed in the corner to help

Additional Layer

The French comic book series called *Asterix* chronicles the struggles of a Celtic village in Gaul as they struggle to resist the Roman advances.

It's not historically accurate, but it is fun.

Famous folks

Brennus was a chieftain of the tribe of Senones who sacked Rome and held the city for ransom in 387 BC. He was expelled by the Roman dictator Camillus.

My Favorite Color Is Plaid!

Celts wore brightly colored fabrics in solid colors, in plaids and tartans, in stripes, and other more complex designs. Their weaving skills were advanced and to the Romans they were gaudy and outlandish looking.

Additional Layer

This statue, *The Dying Gaul,* is a Roman copy of an ancient Greek Statue.

It probably memorializes a victory by the Greeks and possibly also celebrates the bravery and prowess of the Gauls in battle.

Many of the Gauls really did fight naked, while other troops wore light armor.

Fabulous Fact

The Celts were a very war-like people. Prowess in battle was the ultimate desire of a well-brought up Celtic boy. Even their women fought at certain times and places, often as the last line of defense after the men had been defeated. They were head hunters in battle, considering the head the center of the spirit. They would hang the severed heads of their enemies from their horses necks and display them at the entrances to their homes. There is a Celtic Warrior coloring sheet in the printables.

you get started on a nice tight roll. Remove the pen before it disappears inside your paper roll.

Stop rolling when you have just a triangle of paper left. In the center of the roll make a cut in the triangle up to the roll. Tape down the smaller bit of the triangle to the roll to secure it.

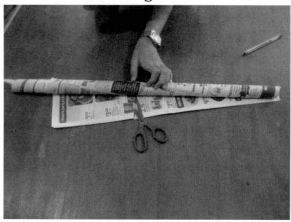

Now cut down the remaining triangle of paper from the center of the tube toward the end until you've cut just over halfway.

Pull the loose flap of the triangle around the handle to make a hand guard. Tape it down.

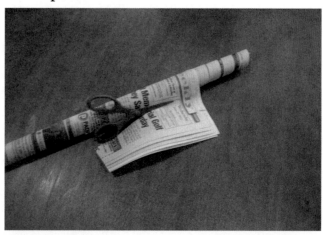

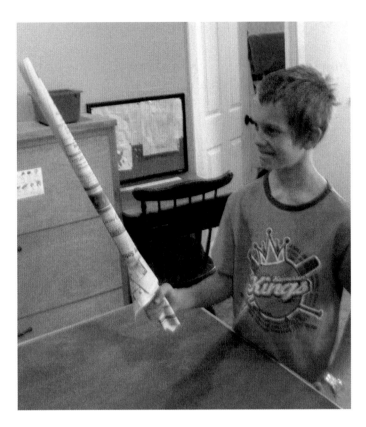

Additional Layer

Among the Celts all trees were sacred, but the most sacred were the oak, ash, and thorn trees. The word "druid" derives from the ancient Celtic word for oak. Trees were thought to be the dwelling places of fairies.

The alphabet used by Irish druids, called the ogham, was thought to have trees as representatives of each of the letters.

Read more about Celtic tree worship. Look for the poem *Cad Goddeu*, an ancient Welsh poem thought to be a remnant of Druidic tree lore.

You can paint your sword out with metallic spray paint or cover it with foil or duct tape.

Write "Vercingetorix, Hero of the Gauls" along the blade.

☺ ☺ ☻ **EXPLORATION: Celtic Myths**
The Celts were famous for their stories. Their myths are a combination of their religion, history, and some good old fashioned storytelling. Find a book of Celtic myths and read several. Choose one that you will learn well and re-tell as a Celtic bard would have. Perhaps the most famous character in Celtic mythology is King Arthur. The Sword in the Stone has been retold and shared countless times, and King Arthur is still considered a hero.

EXPLANATION: Common Mythology
One interesting thing to notice as you study mythology is the commonalities that exist between the stories of peoples across the globe. Often the exact details differ, but there are common threads. Celtic myths speak of "changelings," or mischievous fairies who were swapped with babies at birth. In Ireland these same fairies were called "leprechauns." In still other places they have been called "little people." As you study mythology, look for similarities in other stories you've read.

Fabulous Fact

When you read Irish or Scottish myths and fairy tales you may very well be reading tales that were told thousands of years ago around hearths in little round huts by bards. Many of the tales were written down during the Middle Ages by Christian monks. Often the monks "Christianized" them by adding in little bits and pieces of Christianity, but the basic tales haven't changed in hundreds of years.

Famous Folks

Boudicca was the queen of the Iceni tribe of Britain. She was betrayed by the Romans. She fought back and led her people in revolt. They destroyed Camolodunum, sacked Londinium, and burned Verulamium to the ground killing an estimated 70,000-80,000 people. But then the Romans regrouped and Boudicca's forces were defeated in battle. Rumor has it that she committed suicide rather than be captured by her hated enemies.

A modern rumor has emerged that the final battle took place at King's Cross and that Boudicca's body is buried between platforms 9 and 10.

. . . Perhaps somewhere around nine and three quarters.

Additional Layer

Fiction books by Rosemary Sutcliff regarding this period:

Song For A Dark Queen

Outcast

Tristan and Iseult

The High Deeds of Finn Mac Cool

☻ ☻ EXPLORATION: Druids and Donations

Druids were the priests of the Celts. So little is known about them that some have considered them to be mythological people. They are often mentioned in ancient texts, but no complete descriptions have been made. We do know a few things about Druids. They were religious leaders and were considered to be magical. They were highly respected. They did not pay taxes or serve in the military. They were responsible for organizing religious practices and appeasing the gods through sacrifice. Often this involved offering valuable things to them. For example, a priest may put a sword, jewels, a dead animal, or even a person's body into a sacred pool as a gift to the gods.

Color the picture of the two druids from the end of this unit. Around the druids, write down some things we believe about them.

GEOGRAPHY: EUROPE

Bon Jour! Guten Tag! Hola! Europe is made up of many different countries, cultures, languages, and peoples. Europe is the sixth largest continent in land area, but the third largest in population. It is bordered by the Atlantic Ocean on the west, the Arctic Ocean on the north, the Mediterranean Sea on the south and the Ural Mountains on the east. Europe is really the western end of the huge land mass sometimes called Eurasia. We consider it a different continent because culturally and geographically it is isolated from Asia. The exact borders of Europe in the east are not very well defined and change depending on who you talk to.

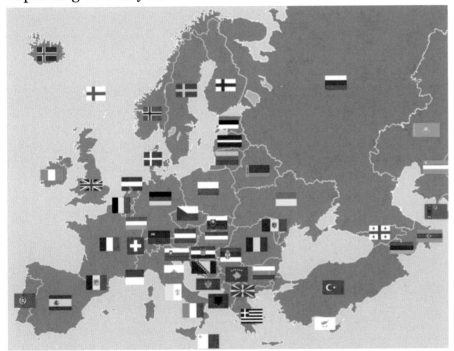

Western culture is descended from the Greeks, Romans, and the kingdoms of Europe. This culture includes the concepts of democracy and republics, Christianity, and many other aspects of our western heritage. Europe is wetter and warmer than the same latitudes in North America because the ocean currents modify its climate. European culture, military, and commerce dominated the world from the Age of Enlightenment until the end of World War II.

Europe is very culturally-rich. It has been the home of the world's greatest artists and musicians. It is full of famous cathedrals, castles, and art museums. Important landmarks like the Parthenon, the Eiffel Tower, the Leaning Tower of Pisa, and Big Ben are also found in Europe.

Additional Layer
Europe is named after Europa, a Phoenician mythological princess who was abducted by Zeus who had taken the form of a white bull.

Enlèvement d'Europe by Nöel-Nicolas Coypel (1726-1727)

Fabulous Facts
The largest city in Europe is Paris with a population of about 10 million.

Europe has a population of about 733 million and shrinking with the lowest birth rate on Earth.

Big Ben is the name of the largest bell in the clock tower at Westminster. Many people mistakenly call the tower "Big Ben." In 2012 the tower was finally named *Elizabeth Tower*.

Writer's Workshop

Europe has several tiny countries including Luxembourg, Andorra, Lichtenstein, Monaco, San Marino, and the Vatican City.

Research more about one of these countries and write about a walk through the country you chose in your writer's notebook.

Additional Layer

There is a sort of "United States of Europe" called the European Union. It includes 27 nations in Europe and is mostly an economic union with a common currency and free trade between the countries. The union also has the power to legislate laws regarding the environment, public health, energy, space exploration, and other functions. It maintains a judicial court system for member nations and has the power to tax the governments of the member states.

As of 2010 or so it is falling apart at the seams as one member nation after another experiences gross failure of financial systems requiring "bail outs" from other disgruntled members.

☺ ☺ ☻ EXPLORATION: Physical Map of Europe

Color and label a physical map of Europe. Use the Europe map from the end of this unit and a student atlas. Include these:
- North European Plain
- Great Hungarian Plain
- Pripet Marshes
- Apennines
- Balkan Mountains
- Crimea
- Jutland
- Kola Peninsula
- Adriatic Sea
- Gulf of Bothinia
- Norwegian Sea
- Barents Sea
- White Sea

☺ ☻ EXPLORATION: United States of Europe

Do you think there could ever be a United States of Europe? Europe is smaller than the the U.S.A., but it is divided into many countries. Why do you think Europe remained divided while the United States established itself as one nation? What are the benefits of each way? Write about it.

☺ ☺ EXPLORATION: Animals of Europe

Many of the animals of Europe are similar to the animals of North America. Choose a species that lives in Europe and write a report about it. You can include pictures of it as well. Go check out this link for a really beautiful European quiet book and some free printable European animal cards:
http://www.imagineourlife.com/2013/11/21/animals-of-europe-for-the-montessori-wall-map-quietbook-with-printables/

☺ ☺ ☻ EXPLORATION: European Feast

Hold a European feast. Choose dishes from various countries throughout Europe to feature at your feast. Here's a possible menu:
- English Fish and Chips
- French Pastries
- German Pretzels
- Spanish Paella
- Italian Pasta

When we held a European feast it was to celebrate the end of our unit on Europe. Each person in our family was assigned a country. They made a flag for the table centerpiece, a poster about their country to share with everyone, and their dish for each person to sample. Each person had time to tell about their country and the dish they prepared.

☺ ☺ ☻ EXPLORATION: Soccer

Soccer is one of the most popular sports around the world, and Europe is no exception to this.

Get some kids together and hold a soccer game just for fun. If you don't have the exact right number of players or all of the equipment, that's okay. A soccer ball and cones for goal posts is all you really need. Go over the rules and then just enjoy the game.

☺ ☻ EXPLORATION: European Flags

Color the flags on the coloring sheet at the end of this unit. This doesn't represent all of the European flags; there are many more. Can you find each flag's nation on a map? Can you spot some European countries that aren't on the coloring sheet?

☺ ☺ ☻ EXPLORATION: Music

Europe has been home to many influential musicians and was the birthplace of some famous instruments like the mandolin, the tambourine, the clarinet, the accordion, and the harp. Color the instruments on the coloring sheet at the end of this unit while listening to some of the classical music of the masters.

Search You Tube to hear some of their beautiful music. You can search for: Beethoven, Mozart, Bach, Brahms, Wagner, Handel, Chopin, Haydn, Strauss, Shubert, and Shumann. There are many, many others as well, but these are some of the best loved.

Ludwig von Beethoven of Germany was one of the most influential and talented musicians of all time.

Additional Layer

The world cup is an international soccer tournament begun in 1930 and held every four years. Italy, Germany, France, England, and Spain are European countries which have won the world cup.

Teaching Tip

As you learn about Europe, put to use the concepts you learned in the past. Look for landforms like peninsulas, fjords, bays, rivers, mountain ranges and so on. Use the global grids and your atlas index to find cities and other places. Use the distribution maps in your atlas or create some of your own. And take note of which biomes can be found in different regions of the continent.

Fabulous Fact

Ancient people defined the eastern edge of Europe at the Don River, which it remained until Swedish geographer von Strahlenberg suggested in 1730 that the Ural Mountains would be a better divider.

Memorization Station

Work to learn as many countries and capitals of Europe as you can manage during this unit. Use puzzles, songs, blank quiz maps, or good old fashioned recitation.

On the Web

Visit: http://www.sheppardsoftware.com/European_Geography.htm

to play an online game that teaches you the geography of Europe.

Additional Layer

Here is a list of the sweeping historical events that have shaped Europe and the west.

Greece

Roman Empire

Christianity

Fall of Rome

Carolingian Renaissance

Italian Renaissance

Colonialism

Enlightenment

Industrial Revolution

Napoleon

Independence Movements

World Wars

Terrorism

☺ ☻ **EXPLORATION: Travel Plans**

Europe is one of the most desirable travel locations because of its beauty, variety, and vibrant history. It is the home to amazing landmarks, museums, and beautiful landscapes. Go talk with a travel agent and get information to plan out a two week vacation to Europe. Decide where you would go and what stops you would make. How many countries could you visit? Where would you stay? What would you need to pack? What would you be eating? How would you get from place to place? Create a detailed itinerary of your travel plans.

☺ ☺ ☻ **EXPLORATION: Country Comparison**

Choose two different European countries. Divide a poster into two columns and write information about each country on each side. You may want to include maps, pictures, graphs, and other visuals you find. Compare their land, climate, culture, cities, traditions, holidays, foods, animals, politics, money, economies, and lifestyles. In what ways are they similar? How are they different?

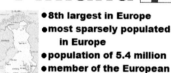

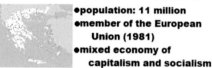

- 8th largest in Europe
- most sparsely populated in Europe
- population of 5.4 million
- member of the European Union (1995)
- Mixed economy of capitalism and socialism

important geographical feature: harsh long winters

Official currency: Euro

- population: 11 million
- member of the European Union (1981)
- mixed economy of capitalism and socialism
- official currency: Euro

important geographical feature: extremely long coast line and innumerable islands.

Greece is the originator of the Olympic Games.

☺ ☺ ☻ **EXPLORATION: Europe Trivia**

Play a fact trivia game to learn more about Europe. Print out and cut apart the cards that you will find at the end of this unit. Look up more facts and add to your trivia game.

SCIENCE: FLOWERING PLANTS

Flowers are the way many plants reproduce. Other plants use spores or cones. Plants produce pollen and egg cells and then pollinate each other to make seeds which are then spread and produce more plants. Plants are pollinated by one or more methods including insect pollination, wind, and animal pollination.

Botanists use many definitions and descriptions to identify plants. Some plants are woody (with hard, bark covered stems or trunks) and some are herbaceous (soft stems). There are different types of flowers: simple, composite, showy, and insignificant. Each of the parts of the flower has a name and function. Leaves are also of different types and may be identified by their characteristics.

An Iris has simple sword shaped leaves with parallel veins running the length of the leaf. An Iris is a monocot. The parallel leaf veining tells us that. The flowers are simple with three sepals and three petals.

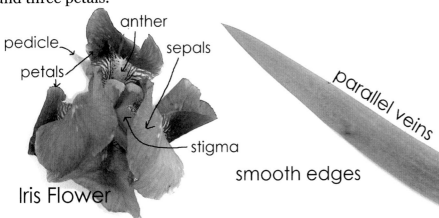

anther
pedicle
petals
sepals
stigma
Iris Flower
parallel veins
smooth edges

Bleeding heart is an herbaceous, soft stemmed plant. The leaves are arranged opposite from one another on the stem. The veins in the leaves are branching, telling us that this is a dicot. The leaves are complexly palmate. Palmate means they spread out like the palm of your hand.

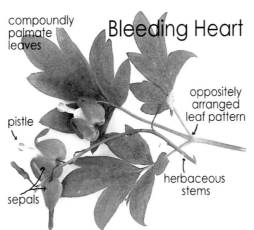

compoundly palmate leaves
Bleeding Heart
pistle
sepals
oppositely arranged leaf pattern
herbaceous stems

Definitions

Monocots, or monocotyledons, are flowering plants that have a single seed leaf, or primal leaf inside the seed. Monocots also have parallel veins running up long narrow leaves. Their petals come in groups of three or multiples of three. Grasses are monocots.

Dicots, or dicotyledons, are flowering plants with two seed leaves inside the seed of a plant. They have branching veins in their leaves. Their flower petals come in fours or fives. Grape plants are dicots.

Writer's Workshop

If you could plant something non-living and make it grow, what would you plant? Don't be obvious and choose a money tree! Be creative and write about what you would plant in your writer's notebook.

Additional Layer

Some plants are parasitic, which means they get their nutrients and energy by stealing it from other plants. Mistletoe is one of over 4,000 types of parasitic plants known. Learn more about how parasitic plants steal their supper.

Fabulous Fact

Pollinators include bees, wasps, hummingbirds, moths, beetles, bats, and humans.

The flowers of the bleeding heart are complex, with the pink sepals taking center stage. The petals are actually small and white and tucked down inside the flower. The stigma pops out of the end of the flower for easy pollination.

Chives have herbaceous stems topped with compound flowers. That means many flowers group together to form the head. A single flower has been plucked from the bunch in the photo below so you can see what one flower on its own looks like.

compound flower head

herbaceous stem with parallel veins

single flower

Chive

Grasses are flowering plants as well, though their flowers are tiny. Grasses are all monocots, with parallel leaf veining. This type of grass has an alternate leaf pattern.

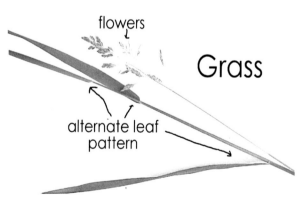

flowers

Grass

alternate leaf pattern

Daisy flowers are actually made up of hundreds of small specialized flowers called florets. The florets around the outside are called ray florets and the yellow flowers in the middle are called disc florets and are where the pollen and egg production happen.

Daisy

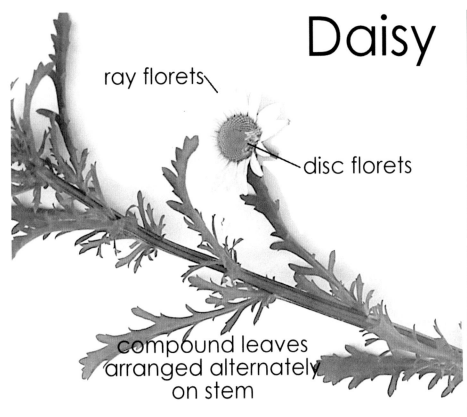

ray florets

disc florets

compound leaves arranged alternately on stem

Lilac bushes have woody stems, simple leaves with smooth edges, oppositely arranged on the stems. The small stem holding the leaf onto the main stem is called a petiole. Not all leaves have petioles; some attach directly to the stem.

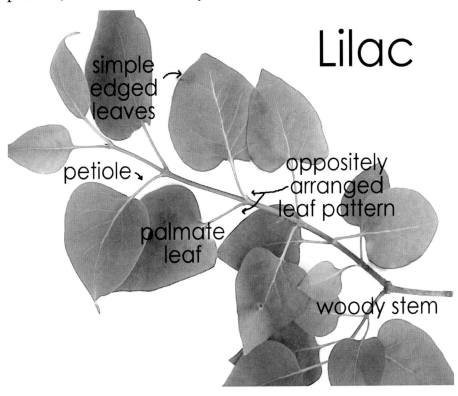

Lilac

simple edged leaves

petiole

palmate leaf

oppositely arranged leaf pattern

woody stem

Photo shared under CC license on Wikimedia.

Additional Layer

The anthers on the end of the pistils contain the pollen for a flower. Learn more about allergies and how pollen and other things can make people sick.

Writer's Workshop

Read *Miss Jaster's Garden* by N.M. Bodecker. A little hedgehog mistakenly gets seeds planted on him and becomes a flower garden. It's a book about the joy of a garden and true respect and friendship.

Then make a book project by planting a little garden of marigolds, baby's breath, and a patch of sweet William. Make up a story of an animal that strays into your garden. What happens to it?

Teaching Tip

Real parents don't always have the time and patience to do all the projects and activities they would like. When all else fails, just read.

☺ ☻ EXPLORATION: Life Cycle of a Flowering Plant

Make a diagram of the life cycle of a flowering plant. You can draw the life cycle or glue seeds and flowers to the paper as well.

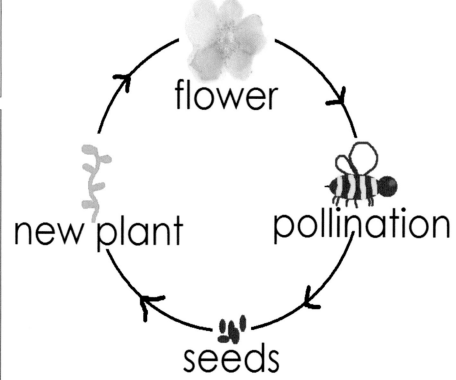

flower

pollination

seeds

new plant

When the plant is pollinated, pollen from the anthers is transferred to the stigma of a different plant of the same species. The pollen travels down the stigma, into the style (the stalk in the center of the plant), and into the ovary. Inside the ovary it meets up with the egg and the two develop into a new seed. Sometimes the ovary develops into a fruit. There are many different types of fruit formations. Look up and research the differences between the ways fruit forms.

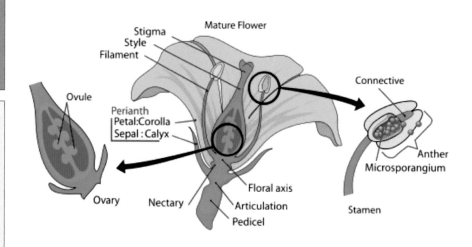

☺ ☺ ☻ EXPLORATION: Plant Collage

Make a plant collage and label different parts and types of plant parts. You could focus on just leaves or just flowers if you like.

☺ ☺ ☻ EXPLORATION: Tissue Flowers

Make a tissue paper flower, plus use this activity to teach about the parts of a flower. It could easily be used for elementary or high school depending on how many parts you expect the kids to memorize.

Materials:

- 7 sheets tissue paper in any color cut into 6 x 12 rectangles
- 1 sheet green tissue paper cut into a 6 x 12 rectangle
- pipe cleaners in yellow, orange, and green

Directions:

1. Lay the sheets of tissue paper on top of each other, with the green on the bottom.

2. Fold the sheets accordion style.

3. Cut the yellow pipe cleaner in half and the orange in thirds. Wrap the yellow pieces around the end of the green, leaving about one and a half inches on the end of the green, so that there are four yellow pieces sticking up. Wrap the orange around the green and yellow join to make one piece of orange sticking up in the center.

4. Wrap the end of the green stem, near the yellow and orange pieces, around the center of the accordion folded tissue paper.

5. Carefully pull up each individual layer of tissue paper to make your flower.

6. Adjust the pipe cleaner pieces so the orange piece sticks up in the center with the yellow pieces surrounding it.

Books Books Books!

One of my favorite books about gardens is *The Secret Garden* by Francis Hodgson Burnett. It makes a great read aloud.

You'll also love *Tom's Midnight Garden* by Phillipa Pierce.

Famous Folks

Theophrastes was an ancient Greek, a student of Aristotle, who wrote two very influential books on plants: *Enquiry into Plants* and *On the Causes of Plants*.

Photo by Singinglemon and shared on Wikimedia.

lours display

and fantasy and

nselfconscious

lding

who

1938

The green pipe cleaner is the stem. The green tissue paper represents the sepals. The colored tissue paper pieces are the petals. The yellow pipe cleaners are the stamens. And the orange pipe cleaner is the pistil.

Older kids can also find the ovary, receptacle, anthers, stigma, style, peduncles and filaments.

You can also get some real flowers and pick them apart and dissect them to find all the parts you learned about. Use a magnifying glass to see better.

☺ ☻ EXPERIMENT: Plant Survey

Do a plant survey like a real botanist out in the field. The purpose is to find out how many of a particular species is present in a particular place or to discover the distribution and populations of many plants in a particular place.

To make your apparatus, you need four straight pieces of 1" wide lumber. We used pre-made picture frame pieces from a craft store for ours. Each piece should be cut into 24" lengths. We bought some that were pre-cut and mitered with the corner pieces that just push together, so no gluing or nailing required.

Next you need twine and flat headed thumb tacks, like those used in quilting. You can find them in the sewing department. From the inside of the frame, measure off five inch sections and place a mark showing where to place your pins. You will end up with four five inch sections and three marks on each side of your frame. Then stretch the twine out across the frame in a grid pattern, as pictured.

To use your plant surveyor, randomly find a place in your yard or in an empty field and place it on the ground. You want a place with several types of plants growing. A lawn with only Kentucky bluegrass would be boring, but my country "lawn," on the other hand, works fabulously. Next, you identify each of the plants inside the grids. The purpose of the grid is to help your eye pick out individual plants, keep you from repeating a particular plant, and confine and put limits on the amount of plants you survey.

Using a piece of graph paper, draw your grid and draw each plant and label it with its name. You may need a plant identification guide to get going. I recommend you start with a place where you know at least most of the plants for your own ease. Like in my "lawn" we have clover, wild daisies, shepherd's purse, dandelions, and the occasional blade of grass, plus a few other things.

Label your graph paper with the place and date where you took your survey. Botanists will do perhaps a dozen or more of these surveys in a field to get a good idea of the plant distribution and population over the whole field. How many you do is up to you. Now you're a real botanist!

☺ ☻ ☻ EXPLORATION: Locals
Identify local plants. It's so cool to be able to look at a tree or plant and just know what it is. It's a skill that before we lived our whole lives indoors, people took for granted. Spend a little time with a good guide book learning at least a few of the common plants around your area. Many areas have plant nurseries that focus on local varieties, or at least have a section in the nursery

Additional Layer
For older kids interested in botany, the plant survey project makes a great beginning to a larger science project. Find an open field and do a complete plant survey of the field. Write up a real scientific paper on the findings complete with graphs and statistics. To find out how to do this, visit http://classweb.gmu.edu /biologyresources/writin gguide/ScientificPaper.ht m from George Mason University. When undertaking a major project of this sort it may be a good idea to contact a biologist or botanist from a university or botanical garden to be a mentor.

Additional Layer
Artists, such as Georgia O'Keeffe, many of the Impressionists and others, painted flowers. Look at some of their art and learn more about them. Try painting a flower yourself.

Japanese Bridge by Claude Monet, 1899

Explanation

Around the house I've set up various areas which I call Exploration Stations. We have a cupboard with science stuff, a drawer with creative writing stuff, an art cupboard, a nature backpack, an astronomy backpack; then there's cooking, water play, play dough, puzzles, plus more.

Michelle

for native plants. They could help you with identification and give you a tour of some native plants in your area.

☺ ☺ ☻ EXPEDITION: Botanical Garden

Visit a local botanical garden. They usually have a section with local native plants. You can learn more about the "weeds" in your garden there.

☺ ☻ EXPLORATION: Plantae

Find a flowering plant from your yard or a nearby park. Find out what it is and discover its Latin name. Use the Latin name and describe the plant in detail in a paragraph or two. See if someone else can tell what plant it is by your description. Be sure to include the leaf shape, number of petals on the flower, type of flower structure, whether it is woody or herbaceous, and other defining characteristics.

☺ ☺ ☻ EXPERIMENT: Attractive Flowers

Flowers are pretty and they smell nice in the garden, but there are other reasons for their existence too. Plants have to be pollinated in order to produce seeds, and for flowering plants this means they need a little help from something with legs or wings. The smell and color of flowers attracts pollinators.

Set up an experiment to see how the color of flowers affects whether pollinators find the flowers.

1. Find three small identical jars or containers
2. Cut out paper flowers from card stock, one red, one white, one green. Cut a hole in the center of the flowers large enough to fit snugly over the opening of the containers you found.
3. Place the paper flowers over the opening of the container and fill the containers half full of sugar water. The water in the containers should be exactly the same.
4. Place the containers outside on a table or patio positioned where you can see them from inside a window.
5. Keep an eye on the containers and note how long it takes bees to find the flowers and which flowers they visit most frequently.

A variation on this experiment is to use a hummingbird feeder with several ports, placing a different colored flower at each port and noting how much use each flower gets.

☺ ☻ EXPERIMENT: Refrigerator Garden

Most of the food we eat comes from flowering plants, whether it's wheat or carrots, apples or potatoes. If you pop a few foods from your fridge into soil and place them on a sunny window they'll sprout and grow.

1. Fill a flower pot or container (it needs holes in the bottom to drain out excess water) ¾ full of potting soil. Wet the soil thoroughly, then let it drain completely into the sink.
2. When it has quit dripping, plant one of these foods from your fridge: grapes, pieces of potato, top inch of a carrot (needs to be whole carrot, not a mangled "baby carrot"), dry beans, dry peas, top ½ inch of a radish, onion, avocado pit, apple seeds, orange pips, or other fruit seeds.
3. See what grows and how long it takes to sprout. We recommend trying more than one type of seed at a time so that if some fail, you'll still have some successes.

Notes:
- Avocados should be planted with the top 1/3 of the seed poking out above the soil. Before you plant, wash the seed and let it dry overnight, then remove the papery seed covering.
- Plants need warmth and water to sprout (and most like it really humid) so place the pot in a windowsill, keep it moist, and cover the pot with a clear plastic bag until you have a few good strong leaves.
- Plants that normally grow in hot places need more heat than average to germinate, place them near the radiator or on top of the warm fridge.
- Some plants can take three or four weeks to sprout so be patient. The quickest ones are carrots and radishes.
- After your plant has sprouted you can call it quits and toss it or you can look up long term care for your plant and keep it alive and maybe even get a harvest.

☺ ☻ EXPLORATION: Pressing Flowers

In Unit 1-16 we taught you how to make a backpack plant press. Press some pretty flowers and make some crafts. Make sure you identify and learn the names of the flowers that you are using.

- Cut out a paper bookmark, cover it with pressed flowers, affix them to the paper with white school glue or decoupage glue, then laminate.
- Make a piece of wall art by gluing pressed flowers to a larger sheet of paper in a design and then frame it.
- Cover a blank book with pressed flowers, coated in decoupage glue to create a diary.

Fabulous Fact

Everything in biology has a long list of vocabulary terms to use and something a simple as fruit is no exception. Here are the parts of a drupe fruit.

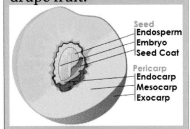

A drupe is a fleshy fruit surrounding a hard pit like a cherry or a peach.

Additional Layer

Where does your fruit come from? Find out where the fruit in your grocery store is grown and find those places on a map.

Fabulous Fact

The art of arranging pressed flowers is called Oshibana in Japan. The artists do not merely arrange the flowers prettily, they create pictures out of them.

Wild Geese by DENG Yingyu and shared under CC license.

Deep Thoughts

Is the tomato a fruit or a vegetable? If you're a botanist, it's a fruit because tomatoes develop from the ovary of a flower. Anything that develops from the ovary of a flower is a fruit and anything that we take from other parts of the plant is not. But we use tomatoes in cooking like a vegetable, so if you're a chef maybe tomatoes are a vegetable after all. Now what about cucumbers and zucchini?

More Experiments

For a variation on the fruit ripening experiment you might leave some of the fruit out on the counter and not in a bag. Does being sealed in the bag have an effect on how quickly the fruit ripens? What if the fruit is inside the refrigerator as opposed to out on the counter?

- Make a pressed flower place mat by gluing your flowers to a large sheet of paper then laminating it.
- Use a candle mold, pressing the flowers to the side with a bit of wax, then pouring the rest of the candle.
- Make gift tags from your pressed flowers by just gluing a single flower to a piece of card stock.

☺ ☺ ☻ EXPERIMENT: Fruit Ripening

Plants produce fruit so that the seeds will be carried off by some animal and distributed far from the parent plant. Fruits develop from the ovary of a flower. As fruits ripen they taste better and better as the starches in the fruit are converted into sugar. You've probably tasted an unripe banana, all woody and pithy and sort of bitter. If you had waited a day the fruit would have been sweet and soft and tasty. The change happens because of a chemical called ethylene. Ethylene is a hormone, a chemical in a living thing that affects the cells in another part of the living thing. Ethylene is released into the air around a fruit that is overripe, or bruised. That's why one bad potato or apple can spoil the whole bushel.

We can test for how ripe a fruit is by testing for starch using iodine. In the presence of starch, iodine turns dark blue-black.

WARNING! Iodine solution will stain anything it touches. Wear gloves and old clothes, and protect your work surfaces! You need:
- unripe pears
- unripe bananas
- iodine solution (Home Science Tools or your pharmacy)
- sealable plastic bags large enough to hold the fruit.

1. Cut one of your pears and one of your bananas into slices.
2. Lay one slice of each into a shallow plastic dish with enough iodine solution to just cover the bottom.
3. Rinse off the fruit slice and take note of how dark it is, you may want to photograph the pieces.
4. Place two unripe pears into a plastic bag and seal. Place two bananas into a plastic bag and seal. Place two pears and two bananas into a plastic bag together and seal.
5. Let the fruit sit out on your counter for 24 hours and then test one banana and one pear from each group for starch again.
6. Let the remaining fruit sit on your counter for one more 24 hour period and test for starch content yet again, taking note of how dark the stain is.

THE ARTS: JEWELRY

Jewelry has been made for centuries across most parts of the globe. Since ancient times people have been creating unique jewelry from metals, stones, shells, beads, and other materials. It is usable, wearable art. It is made to adorn just about every body part, but adornment isn't its only purpose. Jewelry has been used as currency, to show status, and as talismans to either bring luck and fortune, or ward off evil things.

Jewelry is really fun art too, because there aren't rules. You can use anything you want, however you want. You can experiment, play with it, and create whatever you can imagine. By the end of the unit you'll learn a bit about the history of jewelry and also have some cool stuff to wear or give away.

Kenyan Man, image courtesy of Sam Stearman under Creative Commons License.

😊 😊 EXPLORATION: Pasta Beads

To make simple beads for creating your own jewelry you can dye various shapes of pasta noodles and then string them on to yarn or thread. To dye the pasta, mix ½ cup of rubbing alcohol with about 25 drops of food coloring in a plastic zipper bag. Add 3 cups of pasta (you can use a variety of shapes) and swish it around, coating the noodles. Lay it flat and let it sit for 3 hours, swishing and flipping it every 30 minutes. Next, drain the extra alcohol off and let them sit on a cookie sheet until they're totally dry. You can make a variety of colors in different bags.

Fabulous Fact

Jewelry can also show your membership in a group, like Catholics wearing a crucifix or even married people wearing wedding rings.

Additional Layer

This necklace is a modern copy of an ancient Egyptian necklace which is decorated with scarabs, or the images of beetles.

What bug would you put on a necklace?

And this is a Roman snake bracelet. Would you want a snake wound around your wrist?

Additional Layer

Experiment with patterns while making jewelry. In general, a pattern will look more appealing than a random design. Little kids might especially need help with the concept of patterns.

This ancient Egyptian scarab ring has magical symbols of protection carved into the back of it.

Additional Layer

This super fancy Greek earring is of a sphinx. Learn more about a sphinx and see if you can figure out why someone might want to wear one in their ear.

☺ ☺ ☺ EXPLORATION: Egyptians and Their Jewels

In ancient Egypt jewelry manufacturing became a profession for the very first time. The craftsmen, considered to be great artists, used gold and gemstones, which were believed to have magical powers. Write a story about a piece of jewelry that somehow gives you luck and helps you overcome a dilemma. Your story could be set in the past (like in ancient Egypt) or it could be modern-day.

☺ ☺ EXPLORATION: Beaded Bracelets and Necklaces

Most craft stores sell everything you need to make simple beaded bracelets and necklaces. Select your beads. Anything from simple pony beads to fancy glass beads will do. You can buy a variety of clasps, or you can use bracelet elastic and tie it with knots. If you seal each knot with clear finger nail polish it will stay in place and tight.

☺ ☺ EXPLORATION: Greek and Roman Jewelry

The Greeks and Romans made jewelry not as talismans, but to tell stories with. Their jewelry, like much of their art, showed pictures of their myths and stories. Design a piece of jewelry on paper that tells one of the Greek or Roman myths.

☺ ☺ EXPLORATION: Friendship Bracelets

You will need to begin with several colors of embroidery floss, some safety pins, and a pair of scissors. Use the Friendship Bracelet Tutorial Sheet from the end of this unit if you're new to making friendship bracelets. There are also online tutorials.

☺ ☺ ☻ **EXPLORATION: Flip Flops**

Footwear is another accessory that's fun to create. Start with a simple, plain pair of flip flops and add embellishments. Tying or hot gluing items on to the bands of the flip flops is the simplest way. You can use ribbons, fabric scraps, balloons, buttons, flowers, and other embellishments.

☺ ☺ ☻ **EXPEDITION: Renaissance Jewelry**

During the Renaissance jewelry began to be used more and more just for beauty and personal adornment. Jewels were chosen for their attributes of color, luster, and shine rather than for mystical powers. Diamonds became popular, and artisans developed many of the different cuts of jewels that are popular today.

Round   Marquise   Pear   Princess   Heart

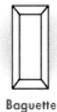

Oval   Emerald   Baguette   Trillion

Additional Layer

Also known as thongs, jandals, slippers, and probably several dozen other names, flip-flops date back at least to the ancient Egyptians. Modern use of this summer footwear can be traced to G.I.'s returning home from Japan after WWII and bringing the Japanese zori with them.

Additional Layer

Button collecting is a popular hobby. In the frugal past our great grandmothers snipped all the buttons from old clothes to save in a button jar. There's even a National Button Society dedicated to preserving, collecting and educating about buttons.

Fabulous Fact

Diamond saws and sandpaper are used to cut gems because diamond is the hardest gem of all. But what do they use to cut a diamond? Another diamond!

Diamond Polisher

Additional Layer

A lot of people think of marijuana when they think of hemp. The two plants are cousins, not the same thing. Hemp has very low levels of the drug that makes marijuana so popular with pot-heads. Hemp is useful mainly for its fiber.

It is illegal to grow hemp in the United States, though the United States is the largest world importer of hemp fiber.

Hemp grows very quickly and requires few pesticides or herbicides. And it can grow well in all but the most dry and cold of climates on Earth.

Writer's Workshop

In books and movies well coiffed heroines often save the day by sacrificing their bobby pins for the purpose of picking locks.

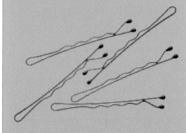

Make up a story where your fabulously jeweled bobby pin saves the day with a well timed escape.

Go to a jewelry store and ask them to show you the different kinds of cuts. Also ask to see some of the different gems. The jeweler can also explain more about jewelry, like what clarity means and what a carat is.

☺ ● EXPLORATION: Button Rings

Simple rings can be made using back loop (shank) buttons and elastic. You simply thread the elastic through the loop on the button and size it snugly to your finger. Overlap the elastic and sew it together, then tuck the sewn edge under the button edge.

☺ ● EXPLORATION: Button Bracelets

To make simple button bracelets, you'll need a variety of large-size 4-hole buttons and two lengths of hemp. Starting from the top, thread the hemp through two holes from top to bottom. Pull the loose ends up through the loop and pull it snugly. Now repeat that with the second piece of hemp through the other two holes. At the back, tie a double adjustable knot so you can adjust the bracelet to get it on and off. See this video on You Tube if you need help tying an adjustable double knot: http://youtu.be/mnft-ewGbqQ.

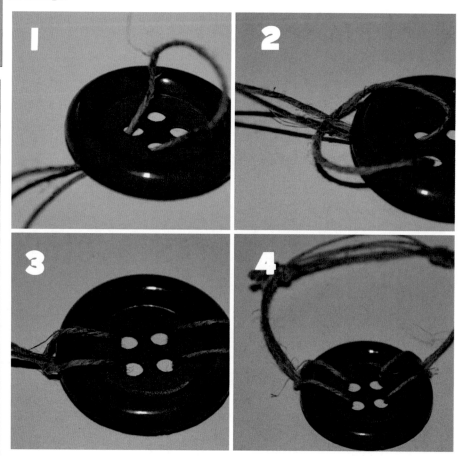

☺ ☺ ☻ EXPLORATION: Hair Pins

Beautiful and simple hair pins can be made with a variety of beads, bobby pins, jewelry wire, and a pair of pliers. Just thread the wire through the beads and tightly around the bobby pins as you go. Tuck the wire ends inside of the beads on the end.

☺ ☻ EXPLORATION: Much Too Much

There are some pretty famous pieces of jewelry out there in the world. Most of the top dollar jewels come from royal families. The necklace that belonged to Marie Antoinette is worth about $3.7 million. It includes many diamonds, including some rare yellow diamonds and a pink diamond.

Additional Layer

Some jewels are famous in their own right like the Hope Diamond, Star of Bombay, Star of India, Jubilee Diamond, Pearl of Allah, Millennium Sapphire, and the Star of Asia. Reading about the pasts of these jewels is reading history.

Writer's Workshop

Pliny, a Roman author and naturalist wrote this about opals:

There is in them a softer fire than the ruby, there is the brilliant purple of the amethyst, and the sea green of the emerald - all shining together in incredible union. Some by their splendor rival the colors of the painters, others the flame of burning sulfur or of fire quickened by oil.

Choose your favorite gem stone and describe it in poetic detail in your writer's notebook.

Additional Layer

Paracord is short for parachute cord and is often called 550 cord by soldiers. This type of nylon rope was first used by parachutists in WWII.

The cord is made of multiple twisted strands of nylon inside a woven nylon sheath. It can be used as a tourniquet, to tie down gear, as a boot lace, as tent or tarp lines, fishing line, sewing thread, for lashing poles together, as a rescue line, and more.

Additional Layer

Besides a paracord bracelet it's a good idea to assemble a survival kit if you're going out in the wilderness. Pack a pocketknife, plastic mirror, whistle, tinder, and waterproof matches or a lighter, first aid kit, bandana, fish hooks, sewing kit, compass and a flashlight into a small bag, then learn how to use each item.

Other Great Jewelry For Boys?

Dog tags; beads on a leather strap for a necklace or bracelet; arrowhead, cross or other pendant on a leather strap; watches, you can even make a homemade band out of . . . paracord.

There have been other jewels that have sold for over $40 million at auctions though, so maybe Marie's is a steal of a deal after all. Do some internet research and see if you can find another historical person whose jewels are now worth much too much.

☺ ☺ EXPLORATION: Hair Flowers

To make simple hair flowers purchase silk daisies, alligator clips, mini brads, and a center (either a button or an acrylic jewel works well). You'll also need a hot glue gun.

Pull apart the flowers, keeping the petals stacked. Put the mini brad through the top of the flower's center and through the top half of the alligator clip. Hot glue a center on top of the flower to finish it off.

☺ ☺ ☺ EXPEDITION: Modern Jewelry

Today jewelry isn't really seen as a sign of wealth because it is so readily available and inexpensive. It is used today for beauty and personal expression.

Do you wear jewelry? What kinds of jewelry describe who you are? Go to a public place, like a park or a shopping mall and look around you. Find people who are wearing jewelry and discuss what their jewelry says about who they are. You don't really know them, but you can make guesses based on their appearance. You might be right, and you might be wrong, but it's interesting to think about the messages we're sending by what we wear.

☺ ☺ ☺ EXPLORATION: Paracord Bracelets

Sometimes these are called survival bracelets, because they can be dismantled for the many feet of rope they are made of. Each single strand of rope is made of many strands, so you can literally end up with hundreds of feet of rope from one small bracelet.

You'll need about 10 feet of parachute cord and a 1" buckle. Loop the cord on to the female end of the buckle as shown, then run the cords through the male end. The length of cord between the buckles will be your finished bracelet length, so you can measure your wrist to figure out how long you want it.

Cobra stitch

Now tie a cobra stitch as shown, and then begin weaving:

At the end you tuck the ends in and then either glue them with hot glue, or fuse them by heating them with a soldering iron and carefully pressing them together. Essentially, you are melting them together, but be careful, because it could burn you.

Entrepreneur

Kurt Walchle claims he made the first paracord bracelet to repair a broken watch band. His friends wanted one too. Eventually they grew so popular that Kurt started a home business called Survival Straps. You can read actual stories of how Survival Straps have saved lives or just helped folks out at:

http://www.survivalstraps.com/pictures-and-stories

Kurt also donates 10% of all proceeds to the wounded warrior project.

Using talents to serve and to make a living. What talents can you turn into a business?

Fabulous Fact

Birthstones date back to the time of Moses when the breastplate of the High Priest was made with twelve colored gem stones representing the twelve tribes of Israel.

Coming up next . . .

Unit 1-18

Roman Republic
Asia - Trees
Roman Art

My Ideas For This Unit:

Title: _____   Topic: _____

_____

_____

_____

_____

_____

_____

_____

_____

Title: _____   Topic: _____

_____

_____

_____

_____

_____

_____

_____

_____

Title: _____   Topic: _____

_____

_____

_____

_____

_____

_____

_____

_____

CELTS – EUROPE – FLOWERING PLANTS - JEWELRY

My Ideas For This Unit:

Title: _____   Topic: _____

_____
_____
_____
_____
_____
_____
_____
_____
_____

Title: _____   Topic: _____

_____
_____
_____
_____
_____
_____
_____
_____
_____

Title: _____   Topic: _____

_____
_____
_____
_____
_____
_____
_____
_____
_____

Celtic Warrior

The Celts were fierce warriors. Their weapons were made of iron and were stronger than the bronze weapons many other groups had. For a time they dominated Europe because of their strong iron weapons and abilities in metalworking. Both men and women fought in war when necessary.

Celts: Unit 1-17

700-500 BC

Hallstatt Celtic culture emerges

600 BC

Celts begin to trade with Mediterranean, Britain is first mentioned as "Albion"

500 BC

Celts arrive in Hibernia (Ireland) from the Iberian Peninsula

400 BC

Celts attack the Etruscans

390 BC

Celts sack Rome, think about occupying, are disgusted by the filth, and demand a ransom instead.

279 BC

Celts invade Greece

275 BC

Celts from Gaul move to Asia Minor, calling it Galatia

230 BC

Galatians defeated by Greeks

200 BC

Celts establish permanent hill forts

121 BC

Rome begins to invade and conquer Celtic Lands

70 BC

Druids from the Middle East arrive in Britain and take over the ruling class

58-51 BC

Julius Caesar defeats Gaul

54 BC

Romans gain a foothold in Britain

79 AD

Roman consolidation of Britain, not including Scotland and Wales

122 AD

Hadrian's Wall built

313 AD

Christianity officially brought to Rome and Roman held Celtic lands

367 AD

Hadrian's Wall falls and Roman decline begins

410 AD

Romans abandon Britain. Celtic people left to defend themselves. They are overrun by Saxons, but resist under a King called Arthur. Celtic cultures in Ireland, Scotland and Wales left intact.

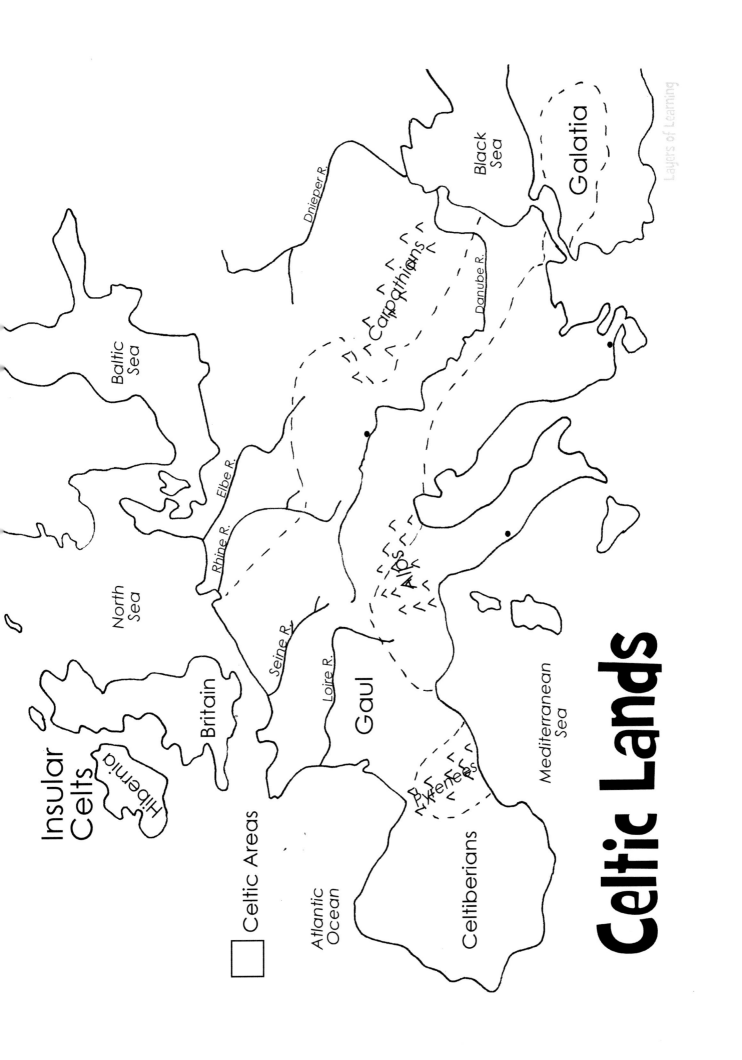

Celtic Lands

Insular Celts

Hibernia

Britain

☐ Celtic Areas

Atlantic Ocean

Gaul

Celtiberians

Pyrenees

Baltic Sea

North Sea

Rhine R.

Elbe R.

Seine R.

Loire R.

Alps

Mediterranean Sea

Dnieper R.

Carpathians

Danube R.

Black Sea

Galatia

CELTIC CALENDAR

An extra, intercalary, month is added every two and a half years to bring the lunar calendar back into line with the solar year. The extra month is inserted after Samonios or after Giamonios. Every month starts on the new moon (when there is no moon) and so the exact date, when compared to our calendar, varies.

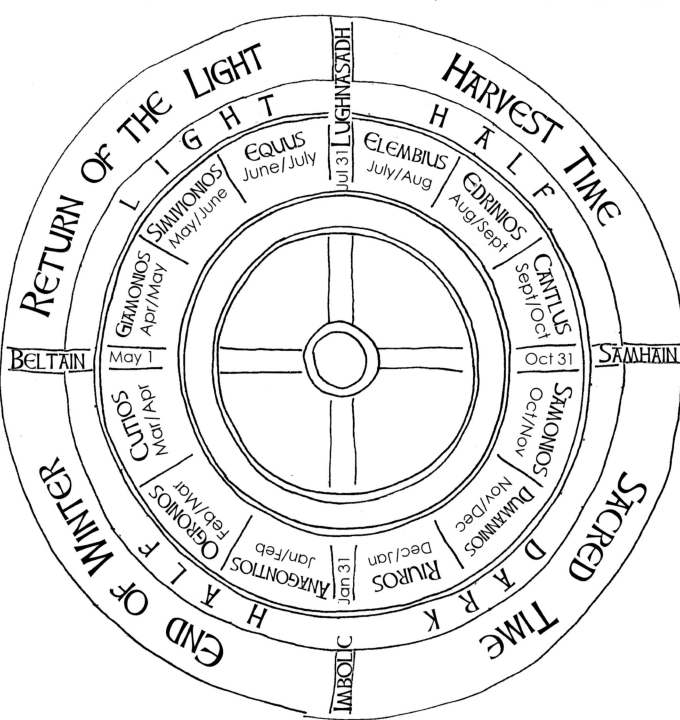

Celtic Druids

Europe

Europe

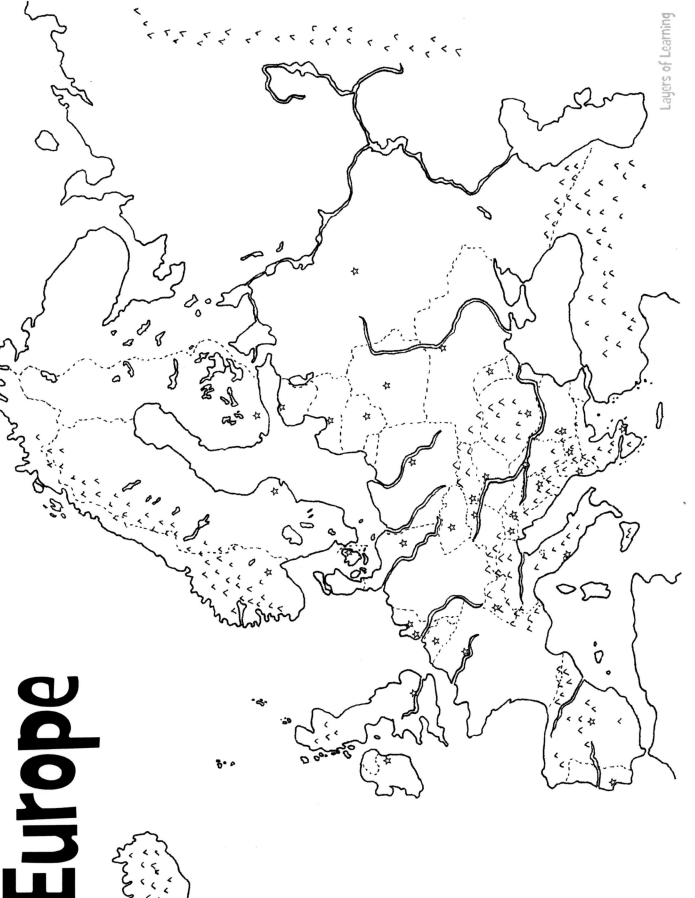

Europe

The smallest country in the world is in Europe, what is it called? *Vatican City*	What is the name of the common currency shared in much of Europe today? *Euro*	Where does the name "Europe" come from? *Europa, who was a Phoenician princess of Greek mythology*	What is the name of the mountain range in northern Italy? *Alps*
What is the largest city in Europe? *Paris*	80 to 90 percent of Europe used to be covered by forests. How much is forested now? *About 25%, mostly in the far north.*	What is a fjord? *Deep winding inlets from the sea cut into a coast, such as the Norwegian coast.*	What is the name of the central lowland plain that covers most of central Europe from France to Russia? *Great European Plain*
Name a desert in Europe. *Hah! Trick question. There are no deserts in Europe.*	Jutland is a peninsula containing what country? *Denmark*	Spain and Portugal are on which peninsula? *Iberian*	Naples, Italy is the same latitude as which American city? *New York*
The Romance languages of Europe are descended from who? *From the Romans, hence Romance . . . it has nothing to do with love.*	What are the three main language groups in Europe? *Romance, Germanic, Slavic*	The Eiffel Tower is located in which country? *France*	What is the approximate population of Europe? *Over 700 million*
Which river in Europe is the longest? *Volva, in Russia*	Which country in Europe has two capitals? *Netherlands: Amsterdam and The Hague*	The zero meridian runs through Europe, what is it called? *Prime Meridian*	Two of the modern wonders of the world are in Europe. What are they? *Chunnel between Britain and France and North Sea Protection works in the Netherlands*

Color the European flags.

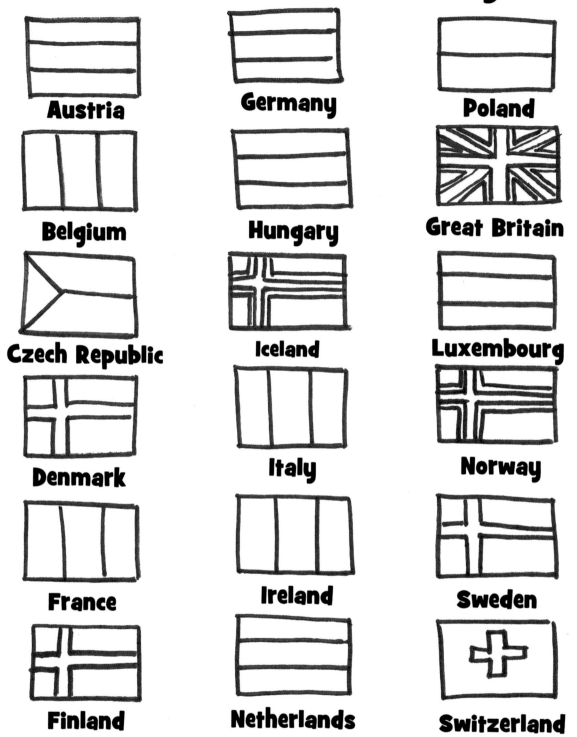

Austria

Germany

Poland

Belgium

Hungary

Great Britain

Czech Republic

Iceland

Luxembourg

Denmark

Italy

Norway

France

Ireland

Sweden

Finland

Netherlands

Switzerland

How many European flags are missing? _____

Color the European instruments.

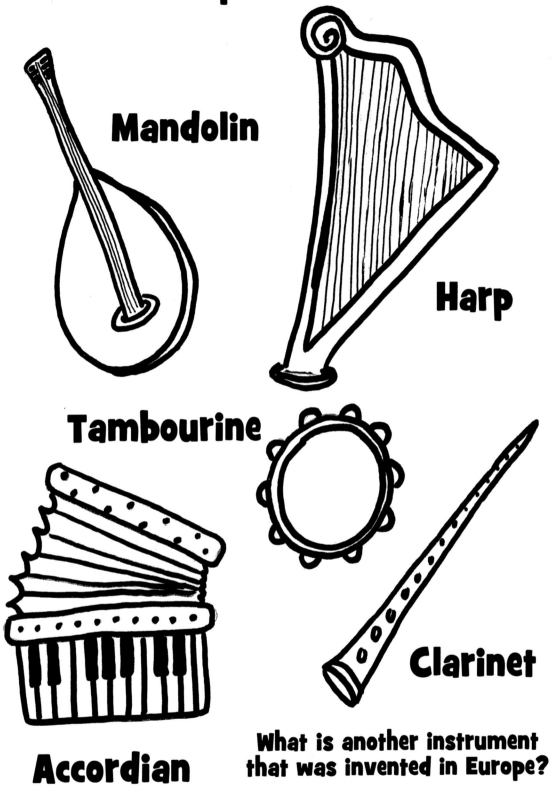

Mandolin

Harp

Tambourine

Accordian

Clarinet

What is another instrument
that was invented in Europe?

_____

Friendship Bracelets

2 Color Half Square Twist With Charms

Colors: A-dark pink, B-light pink, & C-white

1. You will need to cut two 72" lengths each of A & B & two 20" lengths of C. You will also need 2 charms.

2. Put 1 charm on the A threads & the other on the B threads. Fold the A & B threads so they are doubled &, with the charms in the folds, tie all threads together & tape down in this order. Fasten the other ends of the support threads (C) to your shirt. In this design you use 4 threads together like a single thread.

3. Make ½ of a square knot around your support threads. Pull up tight - but not too tight.

4. Work until the length is right. Tie a knot & trim.

Colors: A-white, B-pink, C-green, D-purple, & E-light green

1. You will need to cut two 36" lengths of each color.

2. Tie together & tape down in this order.

3. Start on the left side with A as your knotting thread. Make left knots with A across remaining 9 threads (remember to tie twice).

4. Start again on the left side & make left knots across with the other A.

5. Repeat knots - always starting with the left thread & working left to right. A diagonal pattern will form.

6. Work until the length is right. Tie a knot & trim.

Scrap Spiral

Colors: peach, green, blue, & brown

1. You will need to cut four or five 2-yard lengths of any remaining colors. If some are too short, tie them together to make a longer thread - the knot will not show when you are finished. You can combine colors.

2. Double threads, tie a knot, & tape down. Color order does not matter.

3. Take a double strand of one color & make left knots around the remaining threads.

4. Change the color you are tying with after 1 knot, 2 knots, or just whenever you feel like it.

5. Knot, using left knots all the way, until bracelet is the right length. Tie a knot & trim.

layers-of-learning.com

ABOUT THE AUTHORS

Karen & Michelle . . .
Mothers, sisters, teachers, women who are passionate
about educating kids.
We are dedicated to lifelong learning.

Karen, a mother of four, who has homeschooled her kids for more than eight years with her husband, Bob, has a bachelor's degree in child development with an emphasis in education. She lives in Utah where she gardens, teaches piano, and plays an excruciating number of board games with her kids. Karen is our resident Arts expert and English guru {most necessary as Michelle regularly and carelessly mangles the English language and occasionally steps over the bounds of polite society}.

Michelle and her husband, Cameron, homeschooling now for over a decade, teach their six boys on their ten acres in beautiful Idaho country. Michelle earned a bachelor's in biology, making her the resident Science expert, though she is mocked by her friends for being the *Botanist with the Black Thumb of Death*. She also is the go-to for History and Government. She believes in staying up late, hot chocolate, and a no whining policy. We both pitch in on Geography, in case you were wondering, and are on a continual quest for knowledge.

Visit our constantly updated blog for tons of free ideas,
free printables, and more cool stuff for sale:
www.Layers-of-Learning.com

Made in the USA
Monee, IL
25 August 2020

38516175R00033